Presented by:

_____

To:

_____

Date:

_____

Occasion:

_____

Coming
Together in Joy

"99 Words to Live By"

A series of fine gift books that presents inspirational words by renowned authors and captivating thinkers. Thought-provoking proverbs from many peoples and traditions complete each volume's collection.

"99 Words to Live By" explores topics that have moved and will continue to move people's hearts. Perfect for daily reflection as well as moments of relaxation.

Coming Together in Joy

99 Sayings
by Benedict XVI

edited by

Stephen Liesenfeld

New City Press
Hyde Park, New York

Published in the United States by New City Press
202 Cardinal Rd., Hyde Park, NY 12538
©2007 New City Press

Selection of texts
©2007 Verlag Neue Stadt, Munich, Germany

English translations used with permission
©Libreria Editrice Vaticana

Excerpts from Pope Benedict XVI, *God's Revolution* (San
Francisco: Ignatius Press, 2006), reprinted with permission
from Ignatius Press.

Cover design by Leandro De Leon

Library of Congress Cataloging-in-Publication Data:

Benedict XVI, Pope, 1927-
  [Von der Freude an Gott. English]
Coming together in joy : 99 sayings / by Benedict XVI ;
Stephen Liesenfeld, editor.
    p. cm. -- (99 words to live by)
  ISBN 978-1-56548-273-9 (alk. paper)
1. Benedict XVI, Pope, 1927---Quotations.   2. Christian
life--Quotations, maxims, etc. 3. Christian life--Catholic au-
thors. I. Liesenfeld, Stephen.
II. Title.
BX1378.6.B46   2007
242--dc22   2007022320

Nihil Obstat: William B. Smith, S.T.D., Censor
Imprimatur: Bishop Robert A. Brucato, Vicar General
                  Archdiocese of New York,   May 28, 2007

Printed in the United States of America

Pope Benedict's personal serenity is striking; he exudes a sense of inner peace. No doubt, this is due to the fact that he always tries to listen to the voice of God speaking in today's world. His counsel is distilled from many years of Truth-searching and study, prayer and reflection, priestly ministry and service of the Church. There's something about his gentle, joyful conviction of the truth of faith that attracts us to encounter Jesus once more and so come together in joy.

In his diagnosis of many of our contemporary problems, Pope Benedict comments simply but penetratingly that when God is subtracted from the equation of life and love, something doesn't add up either for us personally or for the world in general. That's why the recovery of our inner hearing and sight has to be a priority in a time of spiritual deafness and blindness.

The 99 sayings in this book are a stimulating invitation to let faith in the God who has taken on a human face in Jesus be reborn in us. They facilitate encounter with him. With a tremendous sense of realism the Pope tells us he knows there have been all kinds of ways that God's image (and with it faith and reason) has been and can be destroyed by hatred and fanaticism. But with fatherly love his meditations encourage us to redirect our gaze to the true face of God.

Pondering these short reflections yields a subtle yet unmistakable sense that Pope Benedict is guiding us on a journey along various aspects of the Christian faith such as the place of reason and faith, Mary, the Eucharist, social justice and evangelization. Ever alert to the real issues of families and young people, priests and teachers, the learned and the simple, the Pope also points us to the way faith can really make a difference in our lives.

It is clear from these pages that in Pope Benedict's faith-vision the Church's identity is one of dialogue with other churches, religions, and with culture. Among the sayings, therefore, we find beautiful reflections addressed to Muslim friends and Jewish brothers and sisters. There are eloquent words too addressed to fellow Christians in the spirit of Jesus' prayer: "May they all be one" (Jn 17:21).

All in all, these 99 sayings provide a concise summary of the main elements of Pope Benedict's teachings. They are a joy to read because they both nourish our spiritual hunger and quench our mind's thirst.

Brendan Leahy

Faith brings us together
and gives us a reason
to celebrate. It gives us joy
in God, joy in his creation,
joy in being together.

In the course of our lives, all of us are on a journey, we are traveling towards the future. Naturally, we want to find the right road: to find true life, and not a dead end or a desert. We don't want to end up saying: I took the wrong road, my life is a failure, it went wrong. We want to find joy in life; we want, in the words of Jesus, "to have life in abundance."

If we follow God
in all that we think and do,
then we draw closer together,
we gain freedom
and thus true
fraternity is born.

The seer of the Book of Revelation is talking about a reconciled world. A world in which people "of every nation, race, people and tongue" (7:9) have come together in joy. And so we ask: "How can this happen? What road do we take to get there?" Well, first and most important: these people are living with God. God himself has "sheltered them in his tent" (cf. 7:15), as the reading says. So we ask ourselves again: "What do we mean by 'God's tent'? Where is it found? How do we get there?" The seer might be alluding to the first chapter of the Gospel according to John, where we read: "The Word became flesh and pitched his tent among us" (1:14).

God is not far from us, he is not somewhere out in the universe, somewhere that none of us can go. He has pitched his tent among us: in Jesus he became one of us, flesh and blood just like us. This is his "tent." And in the Ascension, he did not go somewhere far away from us. His tent, he himself in his Body, remains among us and is one of us.

We can call him by name and speak at ease with him. He listens to us and, if we are attentive, we can also hear him speaking back.

The World Needs God
We Need God

But what God do we need? In the first reading, the prophet tells a people suffering oppression that "He will come with vengeance" (Is 35:4). We can easily suppose how the people imagined that vengeance. But the prophet himself goes on to reveal what it really is: the healing goodness of God. And the definitive explanation of the prophet's word is to be found in the one who died for us on the Cross: in Jesus, the Son of God incarnate, who here looks at us so closely. His "vengeance" is the Cross: a "No" to violence and a "love to the end." This is the God we need.

The Gospel invites us to realize that we have a "deficit" in our capacity for perception. Initially, we do not notice this deficiency as such, since everything else seems so urgent and logical; since everything seems to proceed normally, even when we no longer have eyes and ears for God and we live without him. But is it true that everything goes on as usual when God no longer is a part of our lives and our world?

There is not only a physical deafness which largely cuts people off from social life; there is also a "hardness of hearing" where God is concerned, and this is something from which we particularly suffer in our own time. Put simply, we are no longer able to hear God — there are too many different frequencies filling our ears. What is said about God strikes us as pre-scientific, no longer suited to our age. Along with this hardness of hearing or outright deafness where God is concerned, we naturally lose our ability to speak with him and to him. And so we end up losing a decisive capacity for perception. We risk losing our inner senses. This weakening of our capacity for perception drastically and dangerously curtails the range of our relationship with reality in general. The horizon of our life is disturbingly foreshortened.

The Gospel tells us that Jesus put his fingers in the ears of the deaf-mute, touched the sick man's tongue with spittle and said "Ephphatha" — "Be opened." The Evangelist has preserved for us the original Aramaic word which Jesus spoke, and thus he brings us back to that very moment. What happened then was unique, but it does not belong to a distant past: Jesus continues to do the same thing anew, even today. At our Baptism he touched each of us and said "Ephphatha" — "Be opened," thus enabling us to hear God's voice and to be able to talk to him.

There is nothing magical about what takes place in the sacrament of Baptism. Baptism opens up a path before us. It makes us of the community of those who are able to hear and speak; it brings us into fellowship with Jesus himself, who alone has seen God and is thus able to speak of him (cf. Jn 1:18). Through faith, Jesus wants to share with us his seeing God, his hearing the Father and his conversing with him. The path upon which we set out at Baptism is meant to be a process of increasing development, by which we grow in the life of communion with God, and acquire a different way of looking at man and creation.

Let us ask the Lord with all our hearts to speak anew his "Ephphatha," to heal our hardness of hearing for God's presence, activity and word, and to give us sight and hearing.

Let us ask his help in rediscovering prayer, to which he invites us in the liturgy and whose essential formula he has taught us in the Our Father.

We believe in God. This is a fundamental decision on our part. But again the question has to be asked: is this still possible today? *Is it reasonable?* From the Enlightenment on, science, at least in part, has applied itself to seeking an explanation of the world in which God would be unnecessary. And if this were so, he would also become unnecessary in our lives. But whenever the attempt seemed to be nearing success, inevitably it would become clear: something is missing from the equation! When God is subtracted, something doesn't add up for man, the world, the whole universe.

What came first? Creative Reason, the Creator Spirit who makes all things and gives them growth, or Unreason, which, lacking any meaning, yet somehow brings forth a mathematically ordered cosmos, as well as man and his reason. The latter, however, would then be nothing more than a chance result of evolution and thus, in the end, equally meaningless. As Christians, we say: "I believe in God the Father, the Creator of heaven and earth" — I believe in the Creator Spirit. We believe that at the beginning of everything is the eternal Word, with Reason and not Unreason. With this faith we have no reason to hide, no fear of ending up in a dead end.

The courage to engage the whole breadth of reason, and not the denial of its grandeur — this is the program with which a theology grounded in Biblical faith enters into the debates of our time.

While we rejoice in the new possibilities open to humanity, we also see the dangers arising from these possibilities and we must ask ourselves how we can overcome them. We will succeed in doing so only if reason and faith come together in a new way, if we overcome the self-imposed limitation of reason to the empirically falsifiable, and if we once more disclose its vast horizons. In this sense theology rightly belongs in the university and within the wide-ranging dialogue of sciences, not merely as a historical discipline and one of the human sciences, but precisely as theology, as inquiry into the rationality of faith.

Only thus do we become capable of that genuine dialogue of cultures and religions so urgently needed today.

In the Western world it is widely held that only positivistic reason and the forms of philosophy based on it are universally valid. Yet the world's profoundly religious cultures see this exclusion of the divine from the universality of reason as an attack on their most profound convictions. A reason which is deaf to the divine and which relegates religion into the realm of subcultures is incapable of entering into the dialogue of cultures.

People in Africa and Asia admire, indeed, the scientific and technical prowess of the West, but they are frightened by a form of rationality which totally excludes God from man's vision, as if this were the highest form of reason, and one to be taught to their cultures too. They do not see the real threat to their identity in the Christian faith, but in the contempt for God and the cynicism that considers mockery of the sacred to be an exercise of freedom and that holds up utility as the supreme criterion for the future of scientific research. Dear friends, this cynicism is not the kind of tolerance and cultural openness that the world's peoples are looking for and that all of us want!

The tolerance which we urgently need includes the fear of God — respect for what others hold sacred.

This respect for what others hold sacred demands that we ourselves learn once more the fear of God. But this sense of respect can be reborn in the Western world only if faith in God is reborn, if God becomes once more present to us and in us.

What Do We Actually Believe?

What does it mean to have faith? Is it still something possible in the modern world? When we look at the great Summae of theology compiled in the Middle Ages, or we think of the number of books written each day for or against faith, we might lose heart and think that it is all too complicated. In the end, we can no longer see the forest for the trees. True enough: faith's vision embraces heaven and earth; past, present and future; eternity — and so it can never be fully exhausted. And yet, deep down, it is quite simple. The Lord himself tells us so when he says to the Father: "You have revealed these things to the simple — to those able to see with their hearts" (cf. Mt 11:25).

The Church, for her part, has given us a tiny Summa in which everything essential is expressed. It is the so-called "Apostles' Creed," which is usually divided into twelve articles, corresponding to the number of the twelve Apostles. It speaks of God, the creator and source of all that is, of Christ and his work of salvation, and it culminates in the resurrection of the dead and life everlasting. In its basic structure, the Creed is composed of only three main sections, and as we see from its history, it is merely an expansion of the formula for Baptism which the same Lord entrusted to his disciples for all time when he told them: "Go and make disciples of all nations, baptizing them in the name of the Father and of the Son and of the Holy Spirit" (Mt 28:19).

Faith is simple. We believe in God — in God, who is the Beginning and End of human life. We believe in a God who enters into a relationship with us human beings, who is our origin and our future. Consequently, faith is, always and inseparably, hope: the certainty that we have a future and will not end up as nothing. And faith is love, since God's love is "contagious." This is the first thing: we simply believe in God, and this brings with it hope and love.

The Creed is not a collection of propositions; it is not a theory. It is anchored in the event of Baptism — a genuine encounter between God and man. In the mystery of Baptism, God stoops to meet us; he comes close to us and in turn brings us closer to one another. Baptism means that Jesus Christ adopts us as his brothers and sisters, welcoming us as sons and daughters into God's family. He thus makes us one great family in the universal communion of the Church. Truly, those who believe are never alone. God comes to meet us. Let us go out to meet God and thus meet one another! To the extent we can, let us make sure that none of God's children ever feels alone!

We believe in God. This is what the main sections of the Creed affirms, especially the first section. But another question now follows: in what God? Certainly we believe in the God who is Creator Spirit, creative Reason, the source of everything that exists, including ourselves. The second section of the Creed tells us more.

This creative Reason is Goodness, it is Love. It has a face. God does not leave us groping in the dark. He has shown himself to us as a man. In his greatness he has let himself become small. "Whoever has seen me has seen the Father," Jesus says (Jn 14:9).

God has taken on a human face. He has loved us even to the point of letting himself be nailed to the Cross for our sake, in order to bring the sufferings of mankind to the very heart of God.

Today, when we have learned to recognize the pathologies and the life-threatening diseases associated with religion and reason, and the ways that God's image can be destroyed by hatred and fanaticism, it is important to state clearly the God in whom we believe, and to proclaim confidently that this God has a human face. Only this can free us from being afraid of God — which is ultimately at the root of modern atheism. Only this God saves us from being afraid of the world and from anxiety before the emptiness of life. Only by looking to Jesus Christ does our joy in God come to fulfillment and become redeemed joy.

The second section of the Creed ends by speaking of the last judgment and the third section by speaking of the resurrection of the dead. Judgment — doesn't this word also make us afraid? On the other hand, doesn't everyone want to see justice eventually rendered to all those who were unjustly condemned, to all those who suffered in life, who died after lives full of pain? Don't we, all of us, want the outrageous injustice and suffering which we see in human history to be finally undone, so that in the end everyone will find happiness, and everything will be shown to have meaning? This triumph of justice, this joining together of the many fragments of history which seem meaningless and giving them their place in a bigger picture in which truth and love prevail: this is what is meant by the concept of universal judgment.

We are not meant to waste our lives, misuse them, or spend them simply for ourselves. In the face of injustice we must not remain indifferent and thus end up as silent collaborators or outright accomplices. We need to recognize our mission in history and to strive to carry it out. What is needed is not fear, but responsibility — responsibility and concern for our own salvation, and for the salvation of the whole world. Everyone needs to make his or her own contribution to this end. But when responsibility and concern tend to bring on fear, then we should remember the words of Saint John: "My little ones, I am writing this to keep you from sin. But if anyone should sin, we have an advocate with the Father, Jesus Christ the righteous one" (1 Jn 2:1).

Social Issues and the Gospel
are Inseparable.

When we bring people
only knowledge, ability,
technical competence
and tools,
we bring them too little.

Some people have the idea that social projects should be urgently undertaken, while anything dealing with God or even the Catholic faith is of limited and lesser urgency. Yet ... evangelization itself should be foremost, that the God of Jesus Christ must be known, believed in and loved, and that hearts must be converted if progress is to be made on social issues and reconciliation is to begin....

Love of neighbor, which is primarily a commitment to justice, is the touchstone for faith and love of God. James calls it "the royal law" (cf. 2:8), echoing the words which Jesus used so often: the reign of God, God's kingship. This does not refer to just any kingdom, coming at any time; it means that God must even now become the force that shapes our lives and actions.

When we pray, "Thy Kingdom come," we are not asking for something off in the distance, something that, deep down, we may not even want to experience. Rather, we pray that God's will may here and now determine our own will, and that in this way God can reign in the world. We pray that justice and love may become the decisive forces affecting our world. A prayer like this is naturally addressed first to God, but it also proves unsettling for us. Really, is this what we want? Is this the direction in which we want our lives to move?

Jesus is concerned for the suffering, for those pushed to the margins of society. He heals them and, by enabling them to live and work together, he brings them to equality and fraternity. This obviously has something to say to all of us: Jesus points out to all of us the goal of our activity, how we are to act.

Without Water,
There Is No Life.

People who lived near the desert knew this well, and so springs of water became for them the symbol par excellence of life. The Lamb, Jesus, leads men and women to the sources of life. Among these sources are the Sacred Scriptures, in which God speaks to us and tells us how to live in the right way. But there is more to these sources: in truth the authentic source is Jesus himself, in whom God gives us his very self. He does this above all in Holy Communion. There we can, as it were, drink directly from the source of life: he comes to us and makes each of us one with him.

Through the Eucharist, the sacrament of communion, a community is formed which spills over all borders and embraces all languages.

By making the bread into his Body and the wine into his Blood, Jesus anticipates his death, he accepts it in his heart, and he transforms it into an action of love. What on the outside is simply brutal violence — the Crucifixion — from within becomes an act of total self-giving love. This is the substantial transformation which was accomplished at the Last Supper and was destined to set in motion a series of transformations leading ultimately to the transformation of the world when God will be all in all (cf. 1 Cor 15:28).

In their hearts,
people always
and everywhere
have somehow expected
a change,
a transformation
of the world.

Here now is the central act of transformation that alone can truly renew the world: violence is transformed into love, and death into life.

Since this act transmutes death into love, death as such is already conquered from within, the Resurrection is already present in it. Death is, so to speak, mortally wounded, so that it can no longer have the last word.

To use an image well known to us today, this is like inducing nuclear fission in the very heart of being — the victory of love over hatred, the victory of love over death. Only this intimate explosion of good conquering evil can then trigger off the series of transformations that little by little will change the world.

All other changes remain superficial and cannot save. For this reason we speak of redemption: what had to happen at the most intimate level has indeed happened, and we can enter into its dynamic. Jesus can distribute his Body, because he truly gives himself.

The Body and Blood of Christ are given to us so that we ourselves will be transformed in our turn. We are to become the Body of Christ, his own Flesh and Blood.

We all eat the one bread, and this means that we ourselves become one. In this way, adoration ... becomes union. God no longer simply stands before us as the One who is totally Other. He is within us, and we are in him. His dynamic enters into us and then seeks to spread outwards to others until it fills the world, so that his love can truly become the dominant measure of the world.

The more we allow ourselves, through the liturgy, to be transformed in Christ, the more we will be capable of transforming the world, radiating Christ's goodness, his mercy and his love for others.

"Because there is one bread, we, though many, are one body," says St. Paul (1 Cor 10:17). By this he meant: since we receive the same Lord and he gathers us together and draws us into himself, we ourselves are one.

This must be evident in our lives. It must be seen in our capacity to forgive. It must be seen in our sensitivity to the needs of others. It must be seen in our willingness to share. It must be seen in our commitment to our neighbors, both those close at hand and those physically far away, whom we nevertheless consider to be close.

If the Church tells us that the Eucharist is an essential part of Sunday, this is no mere positivism or thirst for power. On Easter morning, first the women and then the disciples had the grace of seeing the Lord. From that moment on, they knew that the first day of the week, Sunday, would be his day, the day of Christ the Lord. The day when creation began became the day when creation was renewed. Creation and redemption belong together. That is why Sunday is so important.

It is good that today, in many cultures, Sunday is a free day, and is often combined with Saturday so as to constitute a "week-end" of free time. Yet this free time is empty if God is not present.

Sometimes, our initial impression is that having to include time for Mass on a Sunday is rather inconvenient. But if you make the effort, you will realize that this is what gives a proper focus to your free time.

Do not be deterred from taking part in Sunday Mass, and help others to discover it too. This is because the Eucharist releases the joy that we need so much, and we must learn to grasp it ever more deeply, we must learn to love it.

Let us pledge ourselves to do this — it is worth the effort!

Let us discover
the intimate riches
of the Church's liturgy
and its true greatness:
it is not we who are
celebrating for ourselves,
but it is the living God
himself who is preparing
a banquet for us.

Mary is and remains the hand-maid of the Lord who does not put herself at the center, but wants to lead us towards God, to teach us a way of life in which God is acknowledged as the center of all there is and the center of our personal lives.

Mary's Magnificat is a prayer of thanksgiving, of joy in God, of blessing for his mighty works. The tenor of this song is clear from its very first words: "My soul magnifies — makes great — the Lord." Making the Lord great means giving him a place in the world, in our lives, and letting him enter into our time and our activity: ultimately this is the essence of true prayer.

Where God is made great,
men and women are not
made small: there too men
and women become great
and the world is filled
with light.

At the wedding at Cana, Mary makes a request of her Son on behalf of some friends in need. At first sight, this could appear to be an entirely human conversation between a Mother and her Son and it is indeed a dialogue rich in humanity. Yet Mary does not speak to Jesus as if he were a mere man on whose ability and helpfulness she can count. She entrusts a human need to his power — to a power which is more than skill and human ability. In this dialogue with Jesus, we actually see her as a Mother who asks, one who intercedes.

Mary leaves everything to the Lord's judgement. At Nazareth she gave over her will, immersing it in the will of God: "Here am I, the servant of the Lord; let it be with me according to your word" (Lk 1:38). And this continues to be her fundamental attitude. This is how she teaches us to pray: not by seeking to assert before God our own will and our own desires, however important they may be, however reasonable they might appear to us, but rather to bring them before him and to let him decide what he intends to do.

From Mary we learn
graciousness and readiness
to help, but we also learn
humility and generosity
in accepting God's will,
in the confident conviction
that, whatever it may be,
it will be our, and my own,
true good.

Music and song are more than an embellishment (perhaps even un-necessary) of worship; they are themselves part of the liturgical action.... The organ has always been considered, and rightly so, the king of musical instruments, because it takes up all the sounds of creation and gives resonance to the fullness of human sentiments, from joy to sadness, from praise to lamentation. By transcending the merely human sphere, as all music of quality does, it evokes the divine. The organ's great range of timbre, from piano through to a thundering fortissimo, makes it an instrument superior to all others. It is capable of echoing and express-ing all the experiences of human life. The manifold possibilities of the or-gan in some way remind us of the immensity and the magnificence of God.

The pipes of this organ are exposed to variations of temperature and subject to wear. Now, this is an image of our community in the Church. Just as in an organ an expert hand must constantly bring disharmony back to consonance, so we in the Church, in the variety of our gifts and charisms, always need to find anew, through our communion in faith, harmony in the praise of God and in fraternal love.... As the many pipes join together to form one sound, may we as members of your Church be joined together in mutual love and fraternity.

I pray dear friends,
that you will always live
in friendship with Jesus,
so as to know true joy
and communicate it to others,
especially to young people
in difficulty.

I know that you as young people have great aspirations, that
you want to pledge yourselves
to build a better world. Let others see this, let the world see it,
since this is exactly the witness
that the world expects from the
disciples of Jesus Christ; in this
way, and through your love
above all, the world will be able
to discover the star that we follow as believers.

If we think and live according to our communion with Christ, then our eyes will be opened. Then we will no longer be content to scrape a living just for ourselves, but we will see where and how we are needed.

Living and acting thus, we will soon realize that it is much better to be useful and at the disposal of others than to be concerned only with the comforts that are offered to us.

Dear parents!

I ask you to help your children to grow in faith, I ask you to accompany them on their journey towards First Communion, a journey which continues beyond that day, and to keep accompanying them as they make their way to Jesus and with Jesus. Please, go with your children to Church and take part in the Sunday Eucharistic celebration! You will see that this is not time lost; rather, it is the very thing that can keep your family truly united and centered. Sunday becomes more beautiful, the whole week becomes more beautiful, when you go to Sunday Mass together. And please, pray together at home too: at meals and before going to bed. Prayer does not only bring us nearer to God but also nearer to one another. It is a powerful source of peace and joy.

Family life becomes more joyful and expansive whenever God is there and his closeness is experienced in prayer.

Dear catechists and teachers! I urge you to keep alive in the schools the search for God, for that God who in Jesus Christ has made himself visible to us. I know that in our pluralistic world it is no easy thing in schools to bring up the subject of faith. But it is hardly enough for our children and young people to learn technical knowledge and skills alone, and not the criteria that give knowledge and skill their direction and meaning. Encourage your students not only to raise questions about particular things — something good in itself — but above all to ask about the why and the wherefore of life as a whole. Help them to realize that any answers that do not finally lead to God are insufficient.

Dear priests and all who assist in parishes!

I urge you to do everything possible to make the parish a "spiritual community" for people — a great family where we also experience the even greater family of the universal Church, and learn through the liturgy, through catechesis and through all the events of parish life to walk together on the way of true life.

These three places of education — the family, the school and the parish — go together, and they help us to find the way that leads to the sources of life, and truly all of us, dear children, dear parents and dear teachers, want to have "life in abundance."

The briefest description of the priestly mission — and this is true in its own way for men and women religious too — has been given to us by the Evangelist Mark. In his account of the call of the Twelve, he says: "Jesus appointed twelve to be with him and to be sent out" (3:14). To be with Jesus and, being sent, to go out to meet people — these two things belong together and together they are the heart of a vocation, of the priesthood. To be with him and to be sent out — the two are inseparable.

Only one who is "with him" comes to know him and can truly proclaim him. And anyone who has been with him cannot keep to himself what he has found.

We know this from experience: whenever priests, because of their many duties, allot less and less time to being with the Lord, they eventually lose, for all their often heroic activity, the inner strength that sustains them. Their activity ends up as an empty activism.

To be with Christ — how does this come about? Well, the first and most important thing for the priest is his daily Mass, always celebrated with deep interior participation. If we celebrate Mass truly as men of prayer, if we unite our words and our activities to the Word that precedes us and let them be shaped by the Eucharistic celebration, if in Communion we let ourselves truly be embraced by him and receive him — then we are being with him.

The Liturgy of the Hours is another fundamental way of being with Christ: here we pray as people conscious of our need to speak with God, while lifting up all those others who have neither the time nor the ability to pray in this way.

If our Eucharistic celebration and the Liturgy of the Hours are to remain meaningful, we need to devote ourselves constantly anew to the spiritual reading of sacred Scripture; not only to be able to decipher and explain words from the distant past, but to discover the word of comfort that the Lord is now speaking to me, the Lord who challenges me by this word. Only in this way will we be capable of bringing the inspired Word to the men and women of our time as the contemporary and living Word of God.

Eucharistic adoration is an essential way of being with the Lord.... In one of his parables the Lord speaks of a treasure hidden in the field; whoever finds it sells all he has in order to buy that field, because the hidden treasure is more valuable than anything else. The hidden treasure, the good greater than any other good, is the Kingdom of God — it is Jesus himself, the Kingdom in person. In the sacred Host, he is present, the true treasure, always waiting for us. Only by adoring this presence do we learn how to receive him properly — we learn the reality of communion, we learn the Eucharistic celebration from the inside.

Let us love being with the Lord! There we can speak with him about everything.
We can offer him
our petitions,
our concerns,
our troubles.
Our joys.
Our gratitude,
our disappointments,
our needs
and our aspirations.

"The harvest is plentiful" says the Lord. In saying that it is "plentiful," he is not simply referring to that particular moment and to those pathways of Palestine on which he journeyed during his earthly life: his words are valid for today.

They mean that in people's hearts a harvest is growing; they mean, to put it another way, that deep within, people are waiting for God, waiting for a directive full of light to show the way forward, waiting for a message that is more than just words, hoping, waiting for that love which, beyond the present instant, will welcome and sustain us for eternity.

We cannot simply "produce" vocations; they must come from God. This is not like other professions, we cannot simply recruit people by using the right kind of publicity or the correct type of strategy. The call which comes from the heart of God must always find its way into the heart of man. And yet, precisely so that it may reach into hearts, our cooperation is needed. To pray the Lord of the harvest means above all to ask him for this, to stir his heart and say: "Please do this! Rouse laborers! Enkindle in them enthusiasm and joy for the Gospel! Make them understand that this is a treasure greater than any other, and that whoever has discovered it, must hand it on!"

We stir the heart of God. But our prayer to God does not consist of words alone; the words must lead to action so that from our praying heart a spark of our joy in God and in the Gospel may arise, enkindling in the hearts of others a readiness to say "yes." As people of prayer, filled with his light, we reach out to others and bring them into our prayer and into the presence of God, who will not fail to do his part.

The number of priests has declined even if at the present moment we are able to cope, because we have young priests and old priests, and there are young men on their way towards the priesthood. And yet the burdens have increased. To be looking after two, three, or four parishes at the same time, in addition to all the new tasks that have emerged, can lead to discouragement. Often I ask myself, or rather each of us asks himself and his brethren: how are we going to cope? Is this not a profession that consumes us, that no longer brings us joy since we see that whatever we do is never enough? We are overburdened!

Obviously I cannot offer infallible remedies: nevertheless I wish to suggest some basic guidelines. I take the first one from the Letter to the Philippians (cf. 2:5–8), where Saint Paul says to all, especially of course to those who work in God's field: "have in yourselves the mind of Christ Jesus." His mind was such that, faced with the destiny of humanity, he could hardly bear to remain in glory, but had to stoop down and do the incredible, take upon himself the utter poverty of a human life even to the point of suffering on the Cross.

This is the mind of Jesus Christ: feeling impelled to bring to humanity the light of the Father, to help us by forming the Kingdom of God with us and in us. And the mind of Jesus Christ also deeply roots him in all-pervading communion with the Father. An external indication of this, as it were, is that the Evangelists repeatedly recount that he withdraws to the mountain alone, to pray. His activity flows from his profound union with the Father, and precisely because of this, he has to go out and visit all the towns and villages proclaiming the Kingdom of God, announcing that it is present in our midst. He has to inaugurate the Kingdom among us so that, through us, it can transform the world; he has to ensure that God's will is done on earth as it is in Heaven and that Heaven comes down upon earth.

It is necessary to combine zeal with humility, with an awareness of our limitations. On the one hand there has to be zeal: if we truly encounter Christ again and again, we cannot keep him to ourselves. We feel impelled to go out to the poor, the elderly, the weak, to children and young people, to those in their prime. We feel impelled to be "heralds," apostles of Christ.

Yet our zeal, lest it become empty and begin to wear us down, must be combined with humility, with moderation, with the acceptance of our limits. So many things should be done, yet I see that I am not capable of doing them. This is true, I imagine, for many pastors, and it is also true for the Pope, who ought to do so many things! My strength is simply not enough. In this way I learn to do what I can and I leave the rest to God and to my assistants, saying:

"Ultimately you must do this work, Lord, because the Church is yours. You give me only the energy I have. I give it to you, since it comes from you; everything else I place in your hands."

We can serve others
and give to others
only if we personally
also receive, if we do
not empty ourselves.

"Those who believe are never alone." These words apply and must apply especially to priests, to each one of us. They apply in two senses: a priest is never alone because Jesus Christ is always with him. He is with us, let us also be with him! But they must apply in another sense too. He who becomes a priest enters into a presbyterate, a community of priests together with their bishop. He is a priest in this communion with his confrères. Let us commit ourselves to live this out, not only as a theological and juridical precept, but as a practical experience for each of us. Let us offer this communion to one another, let us offer it especially to those that we know are suffering from loneliness, those that we know are troubled by questions and problems, and perhaps by doubts and uncertainties!

A great joy cannot be kept to oneself.... In vast areas of the world today there is a strange forgetfulness of God. It seems as if everything would be just the same even without him. But at the same time there is a feeling of frustration, a sense of dissatisfaction with everyone and everything. People tend to exclaim: "This cannot be what life is about!" Indeed not. And so, together with forgetfulness of God there is a kind of new explosion of religion. I have no wish to discredit all the manifestations of this phenomenon. There may be sincere joy in the discovery. But to tell the truth, religion often becomes almost a consumer product. People choose what they like, and some are even able to make a profit from it. But religion sought on a "do-it-yourself" basis cannot ultimately help us. It may be comfortable, but at times of crisis we are left to ourselves.

Help people to discover the true star which points out the way to us: Jesus Christ! Let us seek to know him better and better, so as to be able to guide others to him with conviction. This is why love for Sacred Scripture is so important, and in consequence, it is important to know the faith of the Church which opens up for us the meaning of Scripture. It is the Holy Spirit who guides the Church as her faith grows, causing her to enter ever more deeply into the truth (cf. Jn 16:13).

"No one has ever seen God; the only Son, who is in the bosom of the Father, he has made him known"; so we read at the end of the prologue of the Fourth Gospel (Jn 1:18). We know who God is through Jesus Christ, the only one who is God. It is through him that we come into contact with God.... In this time of inter-religious encounters we are easily tempted to attenuate somewhat this central confession or indeed even to hide it. But by doing this we do not do a service to encounter or dialogue. We only make God less accessible to others and to our-selves. It is important that we bring to the conversation not fragments, but the whole image of God. To be able to do so, our personal commu-nion with Christ and our love of him must grow and deepen.

We do not fail to show respect for other religions and cultures, we do not fail to show profound respect for their faith, when we proclaim clearly and uncompromisingly the God who has countered violence with his own suffering; who in the face of the power of evil exalts his mercy, in order that evil may be limited and overcome. To him we now lift up our prayer, that he may remain with us and help us to be credible witnesses to himself.

We impose our faith on no one. Such proselytism is contrary to Christianity. Faith can develop only in freedom. But we do appeal to the freedom of men and women to open their hearts to God, to seek him, to hear his voice.

Dear Muslim Friends!
If together we can succeed in eliminating from hearts any trace of rancor, in resisting every form of intolerance and in opposing every manifestation of violence, we will turn back the wave of cruel fanaticism that endangers the lives of so many people and hinders progress towards world peace.

The task is difficult but not impossible. The believer — and all of us, as Christians and Muslims, are believers — knows that, despite his weakness, he can count on the spiritual power of prayer.

The life of every human being is sacred, both for Christians and for Muslims. There is plenty of scope for us to act together in the service of fundamental moral values. The dignity of the person and the defense of the rights which that dignity confers must represent the goal of every social endeavor and of every effort to bring it to fruition. This message is conveyed to us unmistakably by the quiet but clear voice of conscience. It is a message which must be heeded and communicated to others: should it ever cease to find an echo in people's hearts, the world would be exposed to the darkness of a new barbarism. Only through recognition of the centrality of the person can a common basis for understanding be found.

Past experience teaches us that, unfortunately, relations between Christians and Muslims have not always been marked by mutual respect and understanding. How many pages of history record battles and wars that have been waged, with both sides invoking the Name of God, as if fighting and killing the enemy could be pleasing to him. The recollection of these sad events should fill us with shame, for we know only too well what atrocities have been committed in the name of religion. The lessons of the past must help us to avoid repeating the same mistakes. We must seek paths of reconciliation and learn to live with respect for each other's identity.

Christians and Muslims, we must face together the many challenges of our time. There is no room for apathy and disengagement, and even less for partiality and sectarianism. We must not yield to fear or pessimism. Rather, we must cultivate optimism and hope. Interreligious and intercultural dialogue between Christians and Muslims cannot be reduced to an optional extra. It is in fact a vital necessity, on which in large measure our future depends.... I pray with all my heart, dear and esteemed Muslim friends, that the merciful and compassionate God may protect you, bless you and enlighten you always. May the God of peace lift up our hearts, nourish our hope and guide our steps on the paths of the world.

Distinguished Jewish Authorities, Ladies and Gentlemen, dear Brothers and Sisters … *Shalom alêchém!*

The history of relations between the Jewish and Christian communities has been complex and often painful. There were blessed times when the two lived together peacefully, but there was also the expulsion of the Jews from Cologne in the year 1424. And in the 20th century, in the darkest period of German and European history, an insane racist ideology, born of neo-paganism, gave rise to the attempt, planned and systematically carried out by the regime, to exterminate European Jewry. The result has passed into history as the Shoah…. The holiness of God was no longer recognized, and consequently, contempt was shown for the sacredness of human life.

This year, 2005, marks the 60th anniversary of the liberation of the Nazi concentration camps, in which millions of Jews — men, women and children — were put to death in the gas chambers and ovens. I make my own the words written by my venerable predecessor on the occasion of the 60th anniversary of the liberation of Auschwitz and I too say: "I bow my head before all those who experienced this manifestation of the *mysterium iniquitatis*." The terrible events of that time must "never cease to rouse consciences, to resolve conflicts, to inspire the building of peace" (Message for the Liberation of Auschwitz, 15 January 2005). Together we must remember God and his wise plan for the world he created. As we read in the Book of Wisdom, he is the "lover of life" (11:26).

Both Jews and Christians recognize in Abraham their father in faith (cf. Gal 3:7; Rom 4:11ff), and they look to the teachings of Moses and the prophets. Jewish spirituality, like its Christian counterpart, draws nourishment from the psalms. With St. Paul, Christians are convinced that "the gifts and the call of God are irrevocable" (Rom 11:29; cf. 9:6,11; 11:1ff).... Our rich common heritage and our fraternal and more trusting relations call upon us to join in giving an ever more harmonious witness and to work together on the practical level for the defense and promotion of human rights and the sacredness of human life, for family values, for social justice and for peace in the world.

The Decalogue (cf. Ex 20; Dt 5) is for us a shared legacy and commitment. The Ten Commandments are not a burden, but a signpost showing the path leading to a successful life.... My wish is that they [the young people] may be able to recognize in the Decalogue our common foundation, a lamp for their steps, a light for their path (cf. Ps 119:105). Adults have the responsibility of handing down to young people the torch of hope that God has given to Jews and to Christians, so that "never again" will the forces of evil come to power, and that future generations, with God's help, may be able to build a more just and peaceful world, in which all people have equal rights and are equally at home.

Dear Brothers and Sisters in Christ!

Our *koinonia* is above all communion with the Father and with his Son Jesus Christ in the Holy Spirit; it is communion with the triune God, made possible by the Lord through his incarnation and the outpouring of the Spirit. This communion with God creates in turn *koinonia* among people, as a participation in the faith of the Apostles, and therefore as a communion in faith — a communion which is "embodied" in the Eucharist and, transcending all boundaries, builds up the one Church (cf. 1 Jn 1:3).... "So that the world may believe," we must become one: the seriousness of this commitment must spur on our dialogue.

I am quite aware of the painful situation which the rupture of unity in the profession of the faith has entailed for so many individuals and families. This was one of the reasons why ... I declared ... my firm commitment to making the recovery of full and visible Christian unity a priority of my Pontificate.

Together we can rejoice in the fact that the dialogue, with the passage of time, has brought about a renewed sense of our brotherhood and has created a more open and trusting climate between Christians belonging to the various Churches and Ecclesial Communities.... I feel the fact that we consider one another brothers and sisters, that we love one another, that together we are witnesses of Jesus Christ, should not be taken so much for granted. I believe that this brotherhood is in itself a very important fruit of dialogue that we must rejoice in, continue to foster and to practice.

It is obvious that this dialogue can develop only in a context of sincere and committed spirituality. We cannot "bring about" unity by our powers alone. We can only obtain unity as a gift of the Holy Spirit. Consequently, spiritual ecumenism — prayer, conversion and the sanctification of life — constitutes the heart of the meeting and of the ecumenical movement (cf. *Unitatis Redintegratio*, n. 8; *Ut Unum Sint*, 15ff., 21, etc.).

It could be said that the best form of ecumenism consists in living in accordance with the Gospel.

I see good reason in this context for optimism in the fact that today a kind of "network" of spiritual links is developing between Catholics and Christians from the different Churches and Ecclesial Communities: each individual commits himself to prayer, to the examination of his own life, to the purification of memory, to the openness of charity. The father of spiritual ecumenism, Paul Couturier, spoke in this regard of an "invisible cloister" which unites within its walls those souls inflamed with love for Christ and his Church.

I am well aware that many Christians ... expect further concrete steps to bring us closer together. I myself have the same expectation. It is the Lord's commandment, but also the imperative of the present hour, to carry on dialogue with conviction at all levels of the Church's life. This must obviously take place with sincerity and realism, with patience and perseverance, in complete fidelity to the dictates of one's conscience in the awareness that it is the Lord who gives unity, that we do not create it, that it is he who gives it but that we must go to meet him.

I am convinced that if more and more people unite themselves interiorly to the Lord's prayer "that all may be one" (Jn 17:21), then this prayer, made in the Name of Jesus, will not go unheard (cf. Jn 14:13; 15:7, 16, etc). With the help that comes from on high, we will also find practical solutions to the different questions which remain open, and in the end our desire for unity will come to fulfillment, whenever and however the Lord wills. Now let us all go along this path in the awareness that walking together is a form of unity.

Because of the dramatic events of our time, the theme of mutual forgiveness is felt with increased urgency, yet there is little perception of our fundamental need of God's forgiveness, of our justification by him. Our modern consciousness — and in some way all of us are "modern" — is generally no longer aware of the fact that we stand as debtors before God and that sin is a reality which can be overcome only by God's initiative. Behind this weakening of the theme of justification and of the forgiveness of sins is ultimately a weakening of our relation with God. In this sense, our first task will perhaps be to rediscover in a new way the living God present in our lives, in our time and in our society.

Is it not the case today that only through an encounter with Jesus Christ can life become really life? To be a witness of Jesus Christ means above all to bear witness to a certain way of living. In a world full of confusion we must again bear witness to the standards that make life truly life. This important task, common to all Christians, must be faced with determination. It is the responsibility of Christians, now, to make visible the standards that indicate a just life, which have been clarified for us in Jesus Christ. He has taken up into his life all the words of Scripture: "Listen to him" (Mk 9:7).

Let us bear witness
to our faith in such a way
that it shines forth
as the power of love,
"so that the world
may believe" (Jn 17:21).